The problem addressed in Betty Breuhaus's practical and amusing book is: If you don't plan you own funeral, someone else will. It's hard to write breezily about such a dark topic, but When the Sun Goes Down *succeeds, marvelously. There is useful information—you* CAN *avoid singing "Amazing Grace," if you wish—valuable tips, and a tone of informed serendipity that make this book a pleasure to read.*

I wasn't looking forward to my funeral before reading this book ... Well, I'm still not, but now the pill may be a bit easier to swallow.

Alex Beam
Boston Globe columnist

When the Sun Goes Down *is about how to truly celebrate a life well lived. It is hard to imagine how a book about funeral planning can be so much fun to read. But this book is! It is a heartfelt and informative guide that covers the details of end-of-life planning and is interspersed with wisdom, humor, and zest. It is the perfect book for every book club to read and discuss. It is guaranteed to spark wonderful, meaningful conversations with family and friends. No one should wait till the end of his or her life to reflect on what matters. Laugh, learn, and plan your way through this book. Reading it is a gift to yourself and to the people you care about.*

Paula K. Rauch, MD
Director, MGH Cancer Center Parenting Program:
Parenting At a Challenging Time
Massachusetts General Hospital
Harvard Medical School

Ms. Breuhaus presents us with a book ostensibly about death, but actually about life: a book dealing with grief, that dares seek joy. It's a quirky, brave, often funny work, infused with the bracing air of independent thought.

Francis T. Mayo
Estate attorney

I didn't know what to expect when I picked up When the Sun Goes Down, *but immediately I was enthralled in a thoughtful and personal discussion of life, death, and funerals. This book is a valuable resource to stimulate people's thinking about what they want their funeral to be like. A personal celebration and farewell that would epitomize your life, loves, and personality is what most of us desire. Betty Breuhaus shows us how to achieve that goal by preplanning, imagining broad possibilities, and not leaving details to chance. This is a must-read at any age, whether you are young or old. How do you want to be remembered? Beginning with the end in mind is a useful way to think of your life and your last hurrah.*

Judy Waterston
President, Spaulding Rehabilitation Hospital

Betty Breuhaus has presented a difficult subject in an interesting and positive manner. In our lives, we plan many events with our family. Here she provides a guide to help the reader plan their final celebration: their funeral.

Read this guide, involve your family, and consult with your funeral director to plan an event that will reflect your own personal style and, most importantly, help your survivors grieve and celebrate you.

Murphy Family
Murphy Funeral Home

No one's going to the grave with their music still inside them if Betty Breuhaus has her way.

Her gutsy new book cracks open the greatest secret in the world: the process of arranging your own innovative funeral now. It opens the potential to accept your own mortality, and in so doing, creates the potential to live free from fear.

When my beloved father-in-law Corbett Monica died, 300 stand-up comedians and friends came to say good-bye to one of their own. Each took a turn at the microphone, doing bits of their own act, and some blatantly stealing parts of his act. As we laughed and cried our way through our good-byes, we all knew he would not have wanted it any other way.

Real personalized funerals not only look different than traditional funerals, they feel different. The difference is the emotional content. A real personalized funeral is an experience that delivers a powerful personal insight and a powerful emotional connection. It leaves survivors with a strong and lasting sense of who you were to them. It leaves participants with a living and sustainable memory of you that will never die. This is no small gift to give. When accomplished, its effect is felt forever.

If you think you are ready to face one of the most rewarding tasks of your lifetime, let Betty Breuhaus guide you through the development of your own funeral.

It's a must-read for everyone, funeral directors and their advanced-need planners included.

Bill Bates
President, Life Appreciation Seminars

WHEN THE SUN GOES DOWN

WHEN THE SUN GOES DOWN

A SERENDIPITOUS GUIDE TO
PLANNING YOUR OWN FUNERAL

Including a workbook for personal notes
and
a guide for book club discussions

Betty Breuhaus

iUniverse, Inc.
New York Lincoln Shanghai

When the Sun Goes Down
A Serendipitous Guide to Planning Your Own Funeral

iUniverse books may be ordered through booksellers or by contacting:

iUniverse
2021 Pine Lake Road, Suite 100
Lincoln, NE 68512
www.iuniverse.com
1-800-Authors (1-800-288-4677)

Because of the dynamic nature of the Internet, any Web addresses or links contained in this book may have changed since publication and may no longer be valid.

ISBN: 978-0-595-43030-7 (pbk)
ISBN: 978-0-595-87372-2 (ebk)

Printed in the United States of America

Cover design by Geoff Hodgkinson

Front cover photo by Betty Breuhaus

Back cover photo by Barb Engel

Foreword by Dr. Randall H. Niehoff

To

Bill,

Katie,

and the best friends anyone could ever have

When the Sun Goes Down ... it is rising somewhere else. And so goes the cycle of life.

I am standing on the seashore.

A ship spreads her white sails to the morning breeze and starts for the ocean. I stand watching her until she fades on the horizon, and someone at my side says, "She is gone."

Gone where? The loss of sight is in me, not in her. Just at the moment when someone says, "She is gone," there are others who are watching her coming. Other voices take up the glad shout, "Here she comes," and that is dying.

—Henry van Dyke

Contents

Acknowledgments

For their tireless and patient editing of this book, I must thank Katie Kaseler, Susan Bridges, Carol Lacoss, Ran Niehoff, Paula Rauch, Brian Breuhaus, and my most nonjudgmental editor, Apple spell-check. Tombstone drawings were created by Tam Cronin. Many thanks to my husband, Bill Darling, for listening tirelessly to my year-long observations on death.

And, perhaps most importantly, I am extremely indebted to my two constant companions in the office: my golden retriever, Martha May; and my six-foot, life-sized cardboard figure of Red Sox slugger David Ortiz.

Author's Note

Although the word "funeral" is generally used to describe a rite held to mark death with a body present, I have used the word in a broader sense. In my definition, I have included any service, with or without a body present.

The anecdotes found throughout the book are meant to support and clarify the text. While they are all based on true-life experiences, I have taken some liberties in relating them.

Foreword

When the Sun Goes Down offers insightful advice and serves as a handbook for all those who want to take responsibility for the final chapter of their personal lives. This helpful book begins with a focus on planning one's own funeral or memorial celebration but ends up delivering useful tools and warm encouragement to begin experiencing a fuller, happier life today!

Written like the plot of a gripping story, this book actually provides a step-by-step journey for the reader. A creative, energetic, successful businesswoman, wife, and mother, she has done her homework and visited the subject thoroughly. It's as if she has created a *Let's Go ...* guidebook with practical itineraries for thoughtful travelers in this field. And along the way, her narrative sparkles with humor, the anecdotes delight, and the profound quotations she has gathered are, by themselves, worth the price of the book.

The French existentialist Albert Camus, totally absorbed with making the most of the meaning of being a person, taught that "those who do not come to terms with death are unable to fully experience life."

Read this book—enjoy it—it will help you reaffirm the gift of life!

Dr. Randall H. Niehoff
Sr. Minister, Sanibel Congregational United Church of Christ

Introduction

Plan your own funeral??? Perhaps eating aged sushi or being barraged with high-definition techno tunes seem like more attractive alternatives. Why in the world would you do that? You're not dying! Well, I've got news for you! No matter how rich you are, how smart you are, or how powerful you are, no one gets out of this world alive. Even he who dies with the most toys is still dead. Maybe it's time to get off that comfortable couch of denial. Now is the time to put together that inevitable final celebration of your life—your funeral. Take charge, and put together a plan that is so innovative and personal that everyone who attends will feel your very presence and become inspired to live a more worthwhile life. And, while creating this plan, you may find that you have the added benefit of a fresh perspective on your life right now!

Numerous books have been written with standard forms to be filled out and specific instructions to be followed for planning your funeral. *When the Sun Goes Down* makes a giant leap of faith and suggests that you create your very own funeral service. Just as traditional wedding vows did not quite "say it all" at your wedding, and as the traditional "hospital birth" did not suffice for your baby's delivery, neither must you compromise this final celebration of your life with a customary funeral service. You are entitled to make this last celebration of your life entirely your own. The information in this book is meant to spark your imagination and assist you in this exciting and stimulating process.

Traditional funerals are going the way of rotary telephones. Many people are even choosing to forgo funerals on the mistaken assumption that they are unnecessary. The idea that "everyone is suffering enough without all the added confusion" is a terrible misconception, since dealing with grief in a healthy manner is vital. A funeral is an important part of this process. A funeral is *about* the person who has died, but it is really *for* the living. Your loved ones need to gather together to share and support each other in their grief. They need to cry, laugh, hug, and remember together. A funeral is a time for the significance of your life to be celebrated. So why not be the author of this celebration?

Another common misconception is that a funeral is inescapably coupled with a church and clergy. Although this is traditionally the case, it is not compulsory. You are free to personally define exactly the type and style of life celebration you prefer. Spiritual services may be held within church walls or outdoors in a garden. Secular services also can have tremendous power. Personalize this service, and make it your own.

Funerals are often of the cookie-cutter variety. In an emotional turmoil, loved ones call a funeral home, and the details of the service proceed at a rapid and uncontrolled pace. You are given choices, but they are limited and must be made immediately. A wake with an open casket? The deceased dressed in a coat and tie, which is so foreign to him that he is unrecognizable? Everyone gathered in a stuffy little room at the back of the funeral parlor? Canned music? Profuse flowers giving off a sweet and heavy odor? And then a service the next day, in a church the departed would have rather died than attend. Leading the service is a clergyperson who has never laid eyes on the deceased and has to sneak a look at his note cards to reference his name. This is followed by a graveside ceremony featuring a $4,000 casket being lowered into the ground with no one watching.

Then a reception, at either the church or in a dreary function hall. People roam the room uncomfortably, sipping sweet punch and nibbling sandpaper cookies, "comforting" the grieving with such phrases as "He's in a better place now" or perhaps "We'll miss him." Tears are avoided, and eyes are averted. Everyone leaves thinking the survivors are "so strong."

There are many alternatives to this rather maudlin scenario. Now is the time to creatively plan the final celebration of your life. We seem to find plenty of time to anticipate and plan other milestones in life. Weddings, birthdays, and retirement parties are all given lots of thought and preparation. However, the events surrounding a death are certainly not conducive to the same feelings or time frame. The loss of a loved one is a time of stress and grief, regardless of the situation. Often, the pressure of planning a funeral aggravates the survivors so much that they fight among themselves. Each "knew you best" and "knows" what you would have wanted. To present your loved ones with plans to mark this final event is one of the greatest gifts you can give.

Your funeral service should be a reflection of who you were, the people you loved, what you believed in, what you accomplished, and what you did for fun. Did you marry a wonderful woman and share fifty years with her? Tell us what that meant to you. Did you raise wonderful children and do you now have fabulous grandchildren? Tell us how that affected you. Did you volunteer your time and give something back to the community? Tell us how that changed you. What are you most proud of? What was your greatest disappointment? What made you laugh? Did you work to protect the environment? Did you create a garden? Did you golf every conceivable moment you could? Did you know every Red Sox player on the roster? Did you swim every day? Did you have the coolest car on the block? Did you carve wooden eagles? Did you paint? Did you read? Did you write? Reviewing your interests and your values will give you a fresh perspective—and it will give your loved ones a much deeper understanding of you and what made you tick. This funeral will be yours!

Planning your funeral also sets a budget. If you define what you want, no one will have a problem with their conscience later; they will know that you want a plain pine casket and not the eighteen-gauge orchid-brushed casket with a pink velvet interior. They will know your wishes concerning the disposition of your body and will not have to make that very personal decision for you. Nor will they have to guess about the gathering afterward. What would you most like? A formal reception or a picnic in the woods? Champagne and foie gras, beer and sausages, or iced tea and animal crackers? At such a stressful time, articulating your desires makes everyone more comfortable and keeps costs real, without imagined pressure.

Your funeral should be so full of your spirit that your very presence is felt. This service is your final chance to share your life philosophies. People whose lives you have touched will be gathered together. Organizing this service will demonstrate that your caring for them transcends death. Now is the time to pass on worthy lessons and wisdom you have garnered during your lifetime.

Ideally, people will leave this event not only having felt your essence, but also having gained a new perspective on life and how to live it more fully and meaningfully. The ideal funeral will teach the attendees something about living. What a wonderful way to celebrate your life.

Planning your funeral may also have an immediate personal benefit for you. People's attitudes toward death have long been an indication of how they lived. Thinking about death puts a perspective on living. You may gain fresh insights about how you are currently living, which can change your actions and attitudes right now. Americans, in particular, tend to ignore death and not embrace it as a part of life. This attitude can skew both short- and long-term decisions. Sensing that life has a finite end challenges you to stop procrastinating. Do you want to see the coast of Alaska? Go! This perspective might also foster forgiveness and reconciliation. Was that past snub really so cruel and unforgivable? Do you have time to live with it any longer? Come on … let it go.

So go to it! Open your heart and mind to one of life's inescapable sure things. Have the final say. Define your own dignity. Have some fun with it. Take the time to thank and acknowledge the people in your life who have been meaningful. By planning thoughtfully and creatively, you will be giving an invaluable gift to all your loved ones, and you may even change your life in the process.

Death is more universal than life; everyone dies but not everyone lives.

—A. Sachs (1935–), justice, South African Constitutional Court.

1

Benefits of a Funeral

Give sorrow words. The grief that does not speak
Whispers the o'erfraught heart and bids it break.

—Shakespeare (1564–1616), British dramatist, *Macbeth.*

Grief

Omitting a funeral at your death is like removing the spark plug from an engine. Grief is a natural and universal process after a death. Funerals provide the structure to begin a healthy grieving process. You might believe it will be easier on your family if you choose to quietly have your body disposed of, have no service, and have everyone continue with their lives, seemingly untouched by your death,. Though it might be "easier" in terms of less work, a funeral affords a healthier first step in the journey.

Physicians have referred to grief as a hidden illness. A funeral provides a time to grieve and to receive support from friends and family. To deny the pain does not make it disappear; it merely postpones it. The American traditions of sanitizing and avoiding the realities of death are great fodder for therapists, who must help people through their unresolved issues with grief years later. Denial of pain can cause social disorders such as drug or alcohol abuse, as well as other physical maladies. Although grief and tears might appear gauche or "out of control," they are healthy and validate loss. Grief is not the enemy, but rather a healthy and natural process.

Funerals allow people a time to be together, to cry, to hug one another, and to share the loss. A widower needs to be allowed to talk … and talk and talk and talk. A funeral gives people a structure for both offering and accepting comfort, a structure for healthy grief.

> When Barbara's husband died, he had arranged to have no funeral. He didn't want to make it harder on his wife, family, and friends. Barbara had none of the benefits of a funeral and never really accepted his death. She did not move through

1

the progression of healthy grief, and she still cried at the mention of his name until the day she died.

Weeping is perhaps the most human and universal of all relief measures.

—Dr. Karl Menninger (1893–1990), U.S. psychiatrist.

Denial

Where belief is painful, we are slow to believe.

—Ovid (43 B.C.–A.D. 17), Roman poet.

The first stage of grief is denial. A funeral confirms the reality of a death. Viewing the body is, of course, a personal choice. But increasingly, professionals deem it therapeutic for at least those closest to the deceased to view the body. Facing this reality may seem harsh when people are already in pain, but people need reality and closure. Though seemingly illogical, this exposure might well initiate "good grief."

Anna's grief when her six-year-old daughter was struck and killed by an automobile seemed bottomless. When she arrived at the hospital, her precious Cynthia was dead. Doctors, and even her minister, tried to keep her from viewing the body. Because she was so insistent, they finally relented. Later, she recounted the comfort it had given her, as she had imagined it to be so much worse. Reality reins in the imagination.

Establishing the Significance of the Loss

And ever has it been that love knows not its own depth until the hour of separation.

—Kahlil Gibran (1883–1931), Lebanese artist and poet.

A funeral establishes two forms of significance. First, a service defines the loss suffered by the loved ones left behind. When something exciting happens to you, you have a bursting need to tell others. The significance of any event is crucial, be it good or bad. A widow needs to be allowed to talk about her pain and what her husband's death means to her. Listening might not be comfortable for others, but it is vital for her. And secondly, the social significance is established. Your family and friends need to know how much you meant to others. For them to know that others feel a loss is reassuring.

Your loved ones will only truly understand the significance your death has on them after you are gone. It is a time when they will want to tell you something, and you will not be there—a time when they will need comfort, and you will not be not there. If the significance of a loss is not established, the event can become an obsession. Conceivably, twenty years later, a woman might remain fixated on her husband's death, still trying to explain what the loss meant to her. People must be sure that others understand their loss. A good funeral gives people a platform to remember and talk about the departed, to clarify their loss.

You may think that if you don't talk about a loss, a person won't think about it. Wrong. They will, regardless of your conversations with them. They need to talk about their loss. And your sympathy does not make them feel worse. On the contrary, if your sympathy is real, based on understanding, it is a great comfort. It should be noted that it is sympathy, not empathy, that is called for in these situations. Try not to compare a loss you have experienced to another's loss. People are full of their own pain and do not want to have a grief competition. It is imperative that grief not be trivialized. The attempt to "cheer someone up" during this initial grieving process is a big mistake. Grief is not the enemy. Grief should be recognized as natural and healthy.

A funeral also defines the significance the deceased had to the community. The meaning of a person's life may be defined by the memories they leave behind in others. The presence of all the people who take the time to attend a funeral, literally "paying respect," is a wonderful tribute. The worth and significance of the person is clearly in evidence.

> When Carol looked around the room and saw all the people who had come to attend her mother's funeral, her spirit lifted. Family, friends from work, old school chums, neighborhood friends, and church friends were all congregated together. The worth of her mother's life was right there for Carol to see and feel.

Transitional Time

Death ends a life, not a relationship.

—Morrie Schwartz (1916–1995), American educator.

Your funeral is also an important time of transition. A death is not the end of a relationship, but a redefinition of it. You are gone, and your loved ones are left to establish a new relationship with you. For although you are physically gone, your spirit lives on in all these people. They will think of you often. Your presence is now felt through memories. And when they are making decisions that you might have been a part of previously, your input will still be felt. Now your physical being is gone, but your influence is not. The funeral and the gathering afterward are integral parts of this transition.

> A minister was counseling a man whose closest friend, Chuck, had just died. The grief-stricken man listened respectfully, then he suddenly blurted out, "But *where* is Chuck right now?"
>
> The minister sighed and said, "Were you ever really inside Chuck's skin, to know where he was?"
>
> "Well, no," was the reply.
>
> "Then he is right where he has always been for you. He is in your heart. That hasn't changed."

Structure

The very structure of the funeral is helpful to people at a time when their lives are in upheaval. The event provides meaningful and defined activities for people to carry out at a time when self-directed actions are quite difficult. Social roles are defined.

> When Becky and Julia's father died, there were many details that needed to be addressed. People were arriving at the airport, and rooms needed to be arranged, food needed to be prepared, and countless errands needed to be run. As they bounced from one task to another, they had a sense of purpose. They felt that they were actually doing something for their father. The activity was comforting.

Enough said. It is very, very important to your family and friends that you have a funeral. So while you're at it, why not make it a great funeral—a personal funeral that will help them remember you well?

1. Benefits of a Funeral

Considerations

- Begins the healing process for grief
- Makes death real, avoiding denial
- Establishes the significance of the death

  Significance of the loss to survivors

  Significance the deceased had to the community
- Assists with the transitional process
- Gives structure for purposeful behavior

Notes

TO DIE,

IS BUT TO LIVE

FOREVER

Jonathon Mooers
Nantucket, Massachusetts

2

Funeral Homes

Funeral homes can be as disparate in style as Jackson Pollack and Monet. The selection of a funeral home is a key ingredient in the planning process. It is very likely that a funeral home will be involved in at least some aspect of your funeral, although this involvement varies radically. Ordinarily, a funeral home handles (at the very least) the disposition of the body, the death certificate, and other legal documents. On the other hand, a funeral home can handle every detail, from caring for the loved ones at the deceased's side to arranging for transportation to the airport at the funeral's end.

Funeral costs vary widely. Costs may start at $500 and easily go to more than $10,000. Decide what role you want the funeral home to play. One of the most important services a funeral home can provide is support for your survivors. Funeral directors offer knowledgeable emotional support in all kinds of situations. Directors have been through the process countless times and may well have suggestions for circumstances that one would be hard pressed to anticipate. The loss of a loved one is an incredibly emotional time for the survivors. If you have confidence in the funeral director, you will feel reassured, knowing that your family will be dealt with kindly at this difficult time.

Funeral homes can also offer invaluable help in dealing with children. They have materials for talking to children about death and the funeral experience. The sooner a child gains a healthy perspective on the realities of death and its part in life, the better. Make this experience as positive as is appropriate. The knowledge a funeral home has to offer can be quite supportive.

Funeral Home Personalities

Although funeral homes all look quite similar from the outside, each has its own distinct personality. One may be quite grand and elegant, while another is more simple and cozy. Ask friends and acquaintances for recommendations, and learn what your community has to offer.

A funeral director is not necessarily kind and helpful, any more than a doctor is always wise and compassionate. Meet with the personnel at various funeral homes to get to know them. Increasingly, people are choosing the avocation of funeral director later in life. Men and women who have had life experiences with funerals, both good and bad, want to be a part of this process and help others at a difficult time. There is merit in the smaller, privately owned funeral homes. Often these businesses have been family-owned and run for generations, and their personnel are local and active in their communities. It is best to interview more than one funeral director and get a feel for their personalities and accommodations. While their involvement may be minimal or all-inclusive, the funeral home plays a pivotal part in your funeral planning process.

All-Inclusive Packages

Funeral packages can be thoroughly inclusive, offering such services as: helping to notify family and friends, picking up people at the airport, making accommodation plans, providing funeral transportation, coordinating with clergy, arranging flowers, organizing luncheons or gatherings, and even offering legal advice, when appropriate. The funeral director may also plan and deliver the actual funeral service. Again, the funeral home's scope of involvement is your personal choice.

Another option is to not only plan your funeral, but to pay for it in advance as well. One advantage of this approach is that you are locked into the current rates. And, of course, it greatly simplifies everything for your loved ones. However, there are a few considerations to bear in mind. The selected funeral home must still be reputable as well as stable and in business when your time comes. There are also differences in how wisely your prepayment is invested. And in this mobile society, the location of the funeral home must remain convenient for your friends and family. References are available from the National Funeral Directors Association as well as from the Select Independent Funeral Homes organization.

À la Carte

You may also choose to order à la carte from funeral homes. A federal regulation, the Funeral Rule of 1982, requires that funeral homes price each of their goods and services separately so that you know exactly what you are paying for.

Goods sold usually include caskets, urns, and various mementos. Many, if not all, of these goods may be purchased elsewhere. Recently, funeral homes have been unfairly criticized about their pricing, but a good funeral home will have caskets and urns of varying costs, with a wide range of options. The convenience factor should not be overlooked. If the casket is purchased directly from the funeral home, there is much less chance of its not being delivered on time or of its being defective.

Services vary widely and may be selected individually as well. Go through the funeral home's itemized lists of services, and determine which are for you. Making your wishes known now eliminates the potentially guilt-driven, emotional decisions that might be made otherwise.

Your ultimate choice in how you use the funeral home may be based on many criteria. A good funeral director will be more than happy to honor your wishes.

Funeral Home Alternatives

Cemeteries, crematories, and casket stores are beginning to arrange entire funerals. None of these are bound by the same regulations as licensed funeral homes, so it is wise to investigate them even more thoroughly.

When making prearrangements for your funeral, another aspect to consider is that plans made through funeral homes are legally binding and must be carried out. On the other hand, written plans given to survivors are not legally binding and may be changed at will.

Life Appreciation

Another question to ask a funeral home is whether they have participated in the Life Appreciation course given nationwide by Bill Bates, a pioneer in developing personalized services through funeral homes. His ideas are powerful and can be instrumental in training funeral directors to listen and help you create a more beautiful and meaningful service. Rather than doing the "same old, same old" type of conventional service for their clients, Life Appreciation courses are helping funeral directors to plan services that directly reflect the personality of the deceased. Choose the funeral home that is right for you.

> Frank and his father, Frank, Sr., set out to find a funeral home that was just right. It was not unlike the choices that faced Goldilocks. The first home was paneled in a dark wood veneer. It had a maroon shag carpet and a small, dimly lit entrance with artificial flowers. Too somber, they agreed. Next, they encountered a brightly lit room with small pink roses stenciled all around the ceiling. The plastic chairs screeched as they were pulled across the linoleum floor. Marginal, they decided. Finally, they came upon a lovely old building with a dignified entryway leading into a room carpeted with a beautiful oriental rug, and surrounded by heavy brass lighting fixtures. Just right, they concurred!

2. Funeral Homes

Considerations

- Inspect funeral homes
- Consider an all-inclusive package
- Think about à la carte services
- Explore the prepayment option for the funeral
- Look into funeral home alternatives
- Consider the Life Appreciation option

Notes

THE BEST IS YET TO COME

Francis Albert Sinatra

3

Disposition of the Body

Now, what to do with this container you have been living in all these years? One of the most personal decisions you must make is what to do with your body after death. This choice is the most important information to leave in writing to your survivors.

There are two fundamental choices: burial or cremation. Certain religions, such as Orthodox Judaism and Islam, strictly forbid cremation. Most often, however, the disposition of the body is a personal choice.

Both ground burial and cremation advocates claim environmental superiority. Crematoriums are criticized for admitting harmful pollutants into the air, and ground burial advocates are accused of allowing hazardous chemicals from the embalming process into the ground. Pick your poison.

Burial

I could never be buried with people to whom I had not been introduced.

—Norman Parkinson (1913–1990), celebrated English photographer.

The next choice is to decide where you want to be buried. You could choose to be buried underground, or above ground, in a mausoleum. Next is the choice of a burial plot or internment crypt. Different cemeteries have different requirements for what they call "burial vaults." These outer containers hold the original casket and keep the ground from collapsing over time. There are numerous considerations to be addressed.

Sanford and his wife decided to pick out two burial plots. They went to the cemetery and discussed the locations with the manager of the facility. When Sanford inquired who his "neighbors" would be in a particular spot, his wife was horrified. She thought his concern was absurd. Later that week, she mentioned to him at dinner that she had played bridge that afternoon, and the group had decided that

12

they all wanted to be buried next to each other. Hmm … perhaps these thoughts are not quite so incongruous as they might at first appear.

Open/Closed Casket

Since one of the stages in the grieving process is denial, viewing the body can be helpful and can give a sense of "closure." It is a poignant moment when the reality of death is recognized. Often, close family members are present when a loved one dies, and it is very cathartic for them to spend as much time as they deem necessary with the body. Hospitals and those who transport bodies are much more aware of this need than they used to be. It is healthy to use this time wisely. Some people feel that a wider public display of the body in a funeral home is helpful. Still others see no need for any type of viewing, and they maintain that viewing the body is morbid. If the body is present in a closed casket, it is a wonderful opportunity to display a big, beautiful photo or painting of the deceased. Whatever your choice, just be clear that avoiding the viewing is not intended to deny the loss. Again, it is a very personal choice, and there is no right or wrong.

Embalming

If an open casket is used at a funeral home, the body is usually embalmed. Bodily fluids are replaced with preservatives. Embalming was first used in the United States during the Civil War, when soldiers needed to be transported to their homes for burial. Embalming is not an environmentally friendly procedure, as toxic chemicals are used. The United States is the only country where embalming has become customary. It is rarely required by law and provides no public health benefit. Refrigeration is a viable substitute for maintaining a body if a delay in the service is necessary. Make an educated choice.

Caskets

Your choice of casket is limited only by your imagination. Traditionally, a casket is purchased from the funeral home, where they have a variety of choices with different prices. If one of these caskets fills your needs, it is an expedient solution.

Caskets are also available online, with an array of price tags. Trappist Caskets are beautifully constructed wooden caskets made by the monks at New Melleray Abbey from wood that comes from the monastery's own forest. The beautiful workmanship shows a preference for vintage Old World joinery. Or there are discount casket warehouses that carry well-known brands at discount prices. Even Costco has more than a dozen caskets that can be shipped overnight.

If you prefer to use and enjoy your casket prior to your burial, there are more and more opportunities to do just that. A company called Casket Furniture will incorporate the casket's design into a casket sofa or coffin coffee table, or even a casket phone booth. A shop called Heaven on Earth is Britain's first designer death shop. These folks began making what they called "embodiment chests," which were actually dual-function caskets. Coffins were created with game boards inlaid in the top; others doubled as linen chests for storage, bookcases, or CD holders. One custom coffin they supplied was called the Red Arrow jet coffin, designed to authentically replicate one of the Royal Air Force Acrobatic Team; however, the nose and wings had to be detachable, to allow it to fit into the ground. Heaven on Earth has also created a coffin with a ship's wheel on the top. Environmentally friendly caskets are also available. There are two styles of cardboard coffins, a willow coffin, and a bamboo coffin. Customer comments range from "Coffins to die for" to "Heaven on Earth really has put the fun back into funerals."

The Northhouse Folk School in Grand Marais, Minnesota, offers a four-day course in building your own casket, if that interests you. And, of course, caskets can be decorated in any way you wish. A New England Patriots logo can adorn the side. Your school colors and insignia may be your theme. A watercolor of your garden may beautify the sides of your casket. Cowboys can have stirrups for handles. Again, your imagination sets the limits.

It is important to remember that although there are coffins built to last, with liners made of all sorts of materials, nothing is forever. Any container placed in the ground will eventually disintegrate, so don't be fooled by false claims.

> Judy learned that she had a short time to live, so she bought a plain pine coffin and put it in her room. She gathered up markers, paints, and wood burners and invited her friends to help decorate it. Each friend enjoyed a special time with her as they added their personal touch. It was a real tribute to her living memory.

Cremation

Cremation is not a new practice, as there are references to it in both the Old and New Testaments. It is a process by which the body is placed in a retort—a specially designed furnace—and reduced to bone fragments through intense heat. These fragments are further reduced by a pulverizer, which makes them into a consistent powder. The remaining ashes, or cremains, can weigh anywhere from three to nine pounds.

The popularity of cremation in the United States is increasing. In 1950, only 4 percent of the U.S. population chose to be cremated. This number increased to almost 10 percent by 1980, and today it stands at almost 30 percent. It is anticipated that by the year 2025, half of deaths will result in cremation.

People choose cremation for diverse reasons. Some find the substantial monetary savings attractive. Others consider the environmental aspects, citing that ashes require less land use than burials. Others are not comfortable with their body being placed in the earth to decompose. And still others maintain that it both simplifies and dignifies this final event. The practical consideration of transporting a body home from a retirement location is also a factor. Again, it is a very personal decision.

The choice of a reputable crematorium is critical. It may be one affiliated with your funeral home, or you may choose one on your own. If you do not use an experienced funeral home for direction, you can consult the Cremation Association of North America for guidance. There are independent and discounted crematoriums sprouting up around the country. Many stringent policies and procedures are being imposed nationally, as there have been recent cases of these laws being disregarded with rather horrific consequences. You might also want to inquire whether family members may be present during the cremation. Consider your preferences, get references, and investigate the crematorium thoroughly.

A container of some kind is still required for cremation. These containers are available from the funeral home or the cemetery, or they may be purchased on your own. Obviously, this presents a situation where money can be saved by purchasing a very simple casket, since it will not be on display. If a traditional wake with a visitation and open casket is to take place, a casket may be rented for the viewing. Usually, an inexpensive liner is purchased and then placed in a more traditional casket. Again, the funeral home or cemetery would be helpful with this decision.

As funerals become more flexible and religious restrictions diminish, it is probable that cremations will continue to increase.

Urns to Necklaces

Following the cremation, the cremains are given to a predetermined person. Often, the cremains are placed in an urn or other container. Urns have historically been the vessel of choice.

There are Web sites that offer quite diverse receptacles. Urns may be carved from Rocky Mountain aspens from such locations as Silverthorne, Breckenridge, and Telluride. Custom containers in the shape of cowboy boots, golf bags, or race cars are available. Containers may be engraved with the image of a fisherman or a hunter. Urns can be made from many different materials, from bronze to copper, from marble to wood—or even coconut shells. For those who wish never to be separated from their loved one, there are "companion urns" that will hold the cremains of two people. For those wishing to be outdoors, there are wind chimes as well as birdbaths that will hold a portion of your ashes. You might even have a favorite blue bottle on the kitchen windowsill that you would prefer to use to store your human ashes.

Another option is cremation jewelry. Necklaces may be fashioned to hold a portion of ashes around one's neck. For the more affluent, it is possible to take the remaining carbon from cremains and create a low-grade industrial diamond for approximately $2,500. Again, the choices are limited only by your imagination.

Ashes to Ashes

Scattering ashes is an old ritual that offers many alternatives. You may wish to be left in one spot or in a number of locations. Some folks may want to have a portion of their cremains scattered over the mountains where they skied, some alongside a spouse, near their home, and then some over their birthplace. Permission must be granted to leave ashes on public or private property other than your own. Also, scattering ashes at sea is regulated by a federal code, which specifies that they must be thrown into ocean waters at least three miles from shore.

You may arrange to have your cremains placed in a container constructed out of environmentally safe materials and submerged, to become a part of an artificial underwater reef. These reefs are being constructed all over the world to replenish life in the ocean by encouraging the growth of coral.

For the more adventuresome, Space Services Inc. offers the option of being launched into space. A portion of the cremated remains is placed in a flight container. When the date is set for the space shot, families and friends are invited to a pre-launch memorial service and the actual liftoff. A keepsake DVD is also included, as is your biographical sketch on their Web site.

Hunter Thompson, the American journalist, had his ashes blown from a cannon across his ranch in Colorado. And the *Chicago Tribune* ran an article about people who have subtly had their ashes sprinkled over the ivy at Wrigley Field during a Cubs game or while on a tour of the park. Your ashes may be left where your heart once lived.

Donation

We make a living by what we get. We make a life by what we give.

—Sir Winston Churchill (1874–1965), Prime Minister of the U.K.

Donating your body or organs to science after death is becoming increasingly accepted. If you are not working with a funeral home, it is imperative to investigate any institution you are considering. There are numerous agencies that are in place to facilitate whole-body, tissue, and organ donations.

The Anatomy Gifts Registry (AGR) is a nonprofit whole-body donation registry. This organization has hundreds of participating researchers worldwide whose involvement offsets their operating expenses. Not all willed-body donation programs have the stringent guidelines that control this organization. AGR also works with local organ banks to offer organs to the living. The cremated remains of the body are returned within two to four weeks, with no cost to the family.

Medical schools are always in need of body donations. The study of anatomy comes first in many curricula and serves as a foundation for other medical courses. It is increasingly necessary for physicians and biomedical students to conduct special anatomical studies and research. The support from the general public is greatly appreciated. And again, cremains will be returned to the donor's family.

Individual organs may also be donated as transplants to living patients. The U.S. Congress established the Organ Procurement and Transplantation Network (OPTN), which links all the professionals involved in the donation and transplantation system.

LifeLegacy Foundation is a federally approved, nonprofit foundation that accepts organ and tissue donations. These donations are targeted toward the advancement of scientific research and medical education. LifeLegacy will transport the donor from anywhere in the continental United States, file the death certificate, and return the cremated bodily remains within two to three weeks. The foundation even offers a family support coordinator, who assists families before and after the donation. Additionally, there is no cost to the family.

A critical element in the donation decision is communicating your wish to your family. They should understand your beliefs and motives, and hopefully, they will feel a sense of purpose amid their loss.

Importance of Roots

Another consideration to keep in mind is that your survivors may need a place to be "with" you and to celebrate and honor your memory. If so, your bodily remains (or at least a portion of your ashes) should be interred in a mausoleum or buried in the ground somewhere that can actually be visited. It is vital to anticipate the needs of your loved ones when you are gone.

An old monk was once asked why he cared for ancient graves, and why he cleaned the stones to preserve the writings carved there. His reply was simple: "They still have their names. They will always have their names."

—Gregory and Suzanne Wolfe, publishers of the journal *Image*.

3. Disposition of the Body

Considerations

- Decide whether you want to be buried or cremated
- Decide whether you wish to donate your body or parts of your body
- Decide if you want an open or closed casket
- Decide whether you want to be embalmed
- Choose your casket
- Decide what you would like done with your ashes
- Consider a spot where you will be memorialized for your survivors

Notes

Dorothy Cecil
Wimbledon, England c. 1900

4

Cemeteries

All cemeteries are not equal. Cemeteries can be exquisite public parks with rolling hills, panoramic gardens, and beautifully sculpted marble and granite. They are gathering spots where locals may walk and enjoy natural landscapes. Prior to art museums, cemeteries were a kind of "museum without walls," as their carvings and headstones displayed beautiful work. There are any number of reasons why people visit cemeteries. In the historic Oakland Cemetery in Atlanta, folks visit the grave of "Bobby" Jones, the great golfer, and leave golf balls for good luck. And if you pay for a tour of Oakland Cemetery, you will be eligible for five dollars off your bill at Six Feet Under, the catfish restaurant across the street.

For centuries, burials took place in graveyards behind local churches. As space became sparse, the idea of relegating a specific piece of land for burial was created. Within the United States, the first cemetery, from a Greek word for "sleeping place," was Mount Auburn in Boston. In the late nineteenth century, it was one of the most popular tourist attractions in the city. Mount Auburn was the first self-perpetuating rural garden landscape of its type. Paying for a burial plot was a new idea, and as the cemetery flourished and worked economically, others sprang up around the country. When the New York legislature was exploring the idea of creating a park in the center of the city, it was Mount Auburn that was used as a model for Central Park. The legislature proposed that the park be just like Mount Auburn, without the headstones!

Types of Cemeteries

Cemeteries come in many shapes, styles, and sizes. There are profitable, not-for-profit, and government-sponsored cemeteries. Churches and fraternal organizations are likely to own not-for-profit cemeteries. Often, churches also have memorial gardens on their grounds to hold cremains. Municipal cemeteries are run by local government agencies. Private cemeteries sell plots that are run by endowment care funds. If you are considering such a cemetery, investigate these funds, and make certain that they are adequately funded so that they will continue to self-perpetuate after all the plots have been sold. There are also national cemeteries. These plots are available to veterans, their spouses, and usually their minor children. These plots are free; they are given as an honor for military service.

Hollywood Forever in Hollywood, California, is quite an innovative cemetery. Founded in 1899 and formerly known as the Hollywood Memorial Park Cemetery, it holds the remains of Rudolph Valentino, Jayne Mansfield, Tyrone Power, Peter Lorre, and Cecil B. DeMille, among others. The cemetery was left unattended and was in a state of disrepair for years. In 1998, it was purchased and refurbished to its original splendor. Hollywood Forever has introduced some unique services. A funeral service can be viewed worldwide from a Web-based chapel. Hollywood Forever also has a production company that creates LifeStories, a video of your life. These LifeStories are stored in their Library of Lives and may be viewed at any time at various locations throughout the cemetery.

Show me your cemeteries, and I will tell you what kind of people you have.
—Benjamin Franklin (1706–1790), American statesman and inventor.

All-Inclusive Cemeteries

Large corporations are buying up small local cemeteries, and some have started selling not only burial plots, but funeral services as well. They sell caskets and offer funeral services in on-site chapels as well as at the graveside. It is important to know that these cemeteries are not controlled by the same regulations as funeral homes. The full disclosures on price and services imposed on funeral homes are not in effect at these cemeteries.

Green Cemeteries

A new, somewhat radical, and yet very ancient type of cemetery is the burgeoning "green cemetery." In green burials, an unembalmed body is placed in the earth in a biodegradable box or shroud. Green Endings in the United Kingdom manufactures what might well be the most eco-friendly coffin on the market; it is constructed solely of recycled newspapers.

The concept is that the body decomposes, becomes rich fertilizer, and enriches the soil and ecosystem naturally. This environmentally friendly form of burial can actually be used to conserve land. People pay to be buried in a parcel of land, and the money garnered is put toward restoring the remaining land. If customers want any sort of plantings, they have to be native plants. The natural habitat of this open space is thus retained, and it can be used as a park or recreational area. No monuments or markers mar the view. A global positioning system is implemented, to assist visitors in finding their loved ones' burial locations.

The green burial movement started in the United Kingdom and now has approximately 150 sites. There are about twenty green burial cemeteries being developed across the United States. Not surprisingly, northern California is the most active location. Forever Fernwood, a green cemetery being developed in Mill Valley, California, by Tyler Cassity, has received quite a lot of attention. Mr. Cassity maintains that green burial is a vehicle to save the planet. He defines each person as a "tiny little seed bank" in the ecosystem.

It's not enough to be a corpse anymore. Now you have to be a politically correct corpse.

—Thomas Lynch, Michigan funeral director and poet.

Headstones

A headstone marks holy ground where a body is laid and a life is honored. Early headstones were made of slate and often left a moral message. Later, marble was utilized, but it too disintegrated over time. Currently, granite is used, and frequently, the headstones portray some aspect of immortality, such as an obelisk or heavenly looking angels. At the turn of the century, folks could purchase a headstone from the Sears-Roebuck Catalog.

Headstones, or markers, that are flush with the grass are found in memorial parks, which gives an open feeling to the space. Other cemeteries use both flush and upright stones. There are often restrictions on types of headstones allowed in various cemeteries, so consider these regulations when choosing a cemetery.

Although there are traditional headstone styles, there is great potential for personalization. Examples of unique granite memorials abound at Hope Cemetery in Barre, Vermont, next to the Rock of Ages quarries. There is a giant living-room chair, ostensibly representing the deceased's favorite piece of furniture. There are also a granite soccer ball, a race car, an airplane, and even a full-sized bed with two people in it. Create your own. Entire books have been written that provide step-by-step instructions for fashioning long-lasting, beautiful stone monuments. Now, that's personal!

If you don't find it in the index, look very carefully through the entire catalogue.

—Sears-Roebuck Consumer's Guide, 1897.

Epitaphs

If ever there was an opportunity for personalization, it is your epitaph—your final say. Epitaphs give you a measure of immortality, a bridge between you and those to come. The message may be profound or humorous, or it may tell a story. Writing epitaphs was once great fodder for witty parlor games, but today it has come to be considered slightly morbid. Turn back the hands of time, and create some prose for your headstone as a last hurrah.

In lapidary inscriptions a man is not upon oath.

—Samuel Johnson (1709–1784), English author.

4. Cemeteries

Considerations

- Choose a cemetery where you would like to be buried
- Choose a headstone
- Write an epitaph

Notes

I AM READY TO MEET MY MAKER

Whether my Maker is prepared
for the great ordeal of meeting me
is another matter.

Winston Churchill

5

Type of Service

The closest bonds we will ever know are bonds of grief. The deepest community one of sorrows.

> —Cormac McCarthy (1933–), American novelist, *All the Pretty Horses*.

Funerals can be as varied as there are personalities on the planet. Sing your own special song—make it yours. This service should be a reflection of you, your lifestyle, and your personal dignity. An honest and thorough evaluation of your life will be your guiding light in making these decisions.

Funeral services can be held in a church, in a funeral home chapel, by a lake, or in a pub. The body may be present or not; the casket may be open or closed. If cremation is the choice, cremains may or may not be present. The service can be led by the pope, your lifelong minister, a funeral director, a hired celebrant, or a friend. It may take place immediately at your death, or a memorial service may be held later, at any convenient time. Traditionally, memorial services are held without the body present. With so many choices, open your mind, shed conventional wisdom if you like, and create a service that speaks for you.

Church

For many, having a funeral in a church is like having turkey at Thanksgiving. It is quite simply what you do. The clergy from your church or synagogue will traditionally lead the service in your house of worship and, being familiar with you, will be able to put together a meaningful and personal service. However, you certainly still have many choices within this framework.

There are other reasons to have a funeral service in a house of worship. Many people have belonged to a congregation, but they have moved or otherwise lost touch. A return to a former place of worship may offer reassurance and familiarity. Or, if a close relative is comfortable at a particular parish house and you are not averse to the idea, it can be a great comfort to them to be in a recognizable and meaningful place.

After a lovely service in his lifelong, beloved church, with the choir singing all his favorite hymns and his friends reading all his favorite bible passages, Randall's family and friends walked out into the beautiful churchyard. His old kite-flying buddy, Bill, was out there, holding a big, beautiful kite that soared in the air. He invited each of the attendees to stop, take hold of the line, and offer up a silent prayer for Randall. It was a powerful moment for all.

Funeral Home

Another alternative for your service is to use the funeral home as your focal point. Often, funeral homes have small chapels or attractive gathering halls for services. Funeral directors are beginning to offer more and more meaningful and personalized funerals. Courses such as Bill Bates's Life Appreciation Training Seminars train funeral directors to go beyond their traditional roles. Besides being funeral arrangers, they can be personalization specialists. Some funeral directors will even write your entire service or step into the role of master of ceremonies, in conjunction with a clergyperson or other professional.

Some funeral homes are going all-out to create more far-reaching services. One funeral home in the Midwest offers up to fifty different choices for the location of the service; it also offers lists of à la carte options from fireworks to butterfly releases. There is a mortuary in Las Vegas that offers funeral backdrops such as giant playing cards, oversized dice, and a huge slot machine. Even gargantuan casino chips and a "Fabulous Las Vegas" sign are available. Choices abound!

Humanist Services

A humanist funeral service is one that is not centered on a supernatural force. The humanist philosophy rejects the idea of personal immortality and sees death as a real end. Humanists are not averse to emotion at a ceremony, but they do discourage sentimentality and boastful behavior. Humanist philosophy centers on nature, death as a natural process, and the ideals of human living. Humanists maintain that human life on Earth is the supreme goal, rather than an afterlife. While a humanist service is devoid of spiritual references and mention of eternal life, it may still be quite personal and compelling.

Celebrants

Another alternative for your funeral service is to invite a celebrant to officiate. A celebrant is a person—male or female, clergy or layperson—who seeks to meet the needs of families during their time of loss. They provide a funeral service that is personalized to reflect the personality and lifestyle of the deceased.

Celebrants are widespread throughout Australia and New Zealand. Their popularity is growing across the United States, where training is done through Doug Manning's In-Sight Institute. A celebrant plans, writes, and carries out the entire service for the family. Guided by their own code of ethics, celebrants provide top-level and professional funeral services.

At the time of a loved one's death, a celebrant arrives and meets privately with the family for a "storytelling time." By meeting with the family and actively participating, a celebrant creates a safe place for the family's initial grieving process to begin. As the celebrant hears the stories and memories of the deceased, survivors experience a therapeutic effect just by talking. Being encouraged to remember together creates an intimate atmosphere, in which people bond together and begin the new transitions that the death has created.

This family meeting also gives the celebrant a real feeling for the life of the deceased. The celebrant is trained to guide and solicit personal suggestions from families, to help them vocalize the actual significance of the person who has died, and to recognize the importance of participation by loved ones before and during the service. These and other steps begin the healing process right away. The celebrant will then plan, write, and create a service including, when appropriate, readings and words from family members and friends. By incorporating special music, writing the eulogy, and planning ceremonial acts to be used during the service, the celebrant creates a personalized service. If a religious service is planned for the day of the funeral, a celebrant may also conduct a personalized service at the wake the night before. Their flexibility and desire to help out in any way make them invaluable assets.

Celebrants often work with funeral homes, but many are free agents. They can be found through the In-Sight Institute, which certifies celebrants. You would be well advised to find a celebrant who has been certified.

An elderly woman, the mother of five, lived a long and wonderful life and died quietly at home at age eighty-nine. When the children gathered, they remarked that she had very few friends remaining and that there really was not much to say at her funeral. Luckily, one of her offspring had thought to call a celebrant to meet with the group. The more the group talked, the more loving memories they shared. The memory that all of them had in common was of her unbelievably delicious cookies. The celebrant put together a short service that used her recipes as analogies to the other aspects of her life. The children ultimately put together a cookbook of "Mom's Famous Cookies." The inscription inside read, "Mom even smelled like cookies."

Home Death

Anyone who stays away from a death because of distress, because the physical aspects can be so very unpleasant, will turn out to have missed the one experience of a lifetime which can make known the true heights of love.

—Evelyn Francis Capel (1911–), author, priest, and counselor.

One unique variation from the traditional funeral is the rather extreme, yet truly old-fashioned, home death alternative. Rather than having the body immediately handed over to the professional staff of a funeral director at death, the body is cared for by the loved ones at home. This is referred to as "after-death care." The body is either laid in bed or put on display in the parlor, as was the custom years ago. This concept is not dissimilar to the growing practice of choosing to give birth at home rather than at a hospital. Care is provided personally, rather than by a salaried third party.

Caring for a loved one's body for anywhere from one to five days after death gives the family time to assimilate the loss into their lives and assures them that the body is being treated respectfully and lovingly. The body is usually packed in dry ice, and an around-the-clock vigil is kept at the side of the deceased. The term "wake" came from a time when people virtually dropped dead in the fields and were carried into the parlor and laid out. No one was ever entirely certain that the person was indeed dead until days had passed and the person had not reawakened!

With a body at home, people can visit the house, view the body, and have personal time. Obviously, another great benefit is lower cost. At some point, a ceremony can be held, with people gathered around the body. Candle lightings, readings, and music can all be meaningful parts of this time. The body is then removed and either buried, cremated, or donated. For some, this direct involvement in every aspect of caring for their loved ones is a gift and an occasion for healing.

Even with home death, there are reasons to hire a funeral home to handle details such as death certificates and other legal matters. However, the law does not require professionals to do these tasks. If you wish, the instructions for handling this process may be left with your survivors. Lisa Carlson has written a book, *Caring for Your Own Dead*, with many poignant examples of this ritual as well as detailed information on regulations, state by state. Two organizations, Crossings and Final Passages, are quite involved with the home death experience, and they have extensive and detailed information on dealing with after-death care at home.

When Steve died at the age of eighty-one, his neighbors and friends went to his home to pay their respects to his widow and children. Many were a bit taken aback to learn that they could also pay their respects to Steve at the same time. His body lay on his bed in the master bedroom, dressed in his favorite fishing clothes, surrounded by flowers and burning candles, with his favorite classical music selections playing. His wife, Arlene, had made the decision to care for him after his death. After three days of grieving at home, she felt she was ready to let go of his body. She understood and accepted the finality and reality of his death. She found caring for Steve to be a rewarding final act of love.

Viking Funerals

If you have a sense of the dramatic, and cling hard and fast to ancient traditions, a Viking funeral might be a perfect choice. The Vikings believed that this funeral form guaranteed immortality. A corpse is loaded into a ship or smaller craft, as monetary restrictions dictate. The boat is pushed off from shore at sunset and lit on fire with a flaming arrow. If the color of the fire and the sunset match, it proves that the deceased led a good life.

This type of funeral appeared quite appealing in the 1988 film *Rocket Gibraltar* with Burt Lancaster, but it may leave something to be desired in actual practice. It's good to keep an open mind, though.

The art of living well and the art of dying well are one.

—Epicurus (341 B.C.–270 B.C.), Greek philosopher.

5. Type of Service

Considerations

- Decide whether you want a traditional church funeral
- Consider whether you would prefer to hold your funeral in a funeral home
- Choose a unique location where you would like your service to be held
- Consider whether a humanist service is appropriate
- Look into using a celebrant to officiate
- Think about whether you would prefer to have a home death
- Investigate having a Viking funeral

Notes

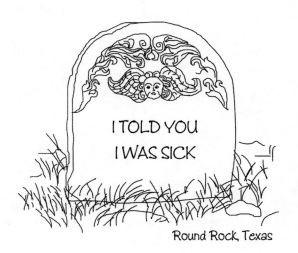

I TOLD YOU
I WAS SICK

Round Rock, Texas

6

Fundamentals

Planning your actual funeral service may seem a bit daunting. But, as with most things, if you just begin at the beginning and develop ideas around a core, it will build on itself and become clear to you as you go along.

Personal Particulars

Details create the big picture.

—Sanford I. Weill (1933–), banker and financier.

Since one of your key intentions is to aid your loved ones with details concerning your funeral, it is important to leave them with the vital details of your life. The real nuts and bolts of your days need to be in written form and accessible to those who will need it.

There are many formal documents available that articulate exactly what information is necessary for your loved ones. These forms are available at funeral homes, from local religious organizations, and online. There are also entire books offering guidance in accomplishing these details. The minimal time it will take you to fill out such forms will save much time for your survivors.

Another thoughtful detail to include is a list of who should be contacted at your death. It will not be an easy time for your family, and any detail that gives them relief and helps them to avoid unconscious slights will be invaluable.

Here are examples of required information:

Personal History

Full Name: Maiden Name:

Address: City: State: Zip:

Telephone:

Birthplace: Date of Birth:

Social Security Number:

Marital Status: Married/Single/Divorced/Widowed/Never Married

Spouse:

Father's Name:

Mother's Name: Maiden Name:

Children:

Stepchildren:

Education:

Occupation:

Religious Affiliation:

Military Information:

Clubs and Organizations:

Personal Records

Bank Accounts:

Safe Deposit Box: Location of Key:

Insurance Policies:

Real Estate:

Stocks and Bonds:

Assets and Liabilities:

Leave this information with a trusted member of your family ... or two!

> *Let each of us become all that he was created capable of being.*
>
> —Thomas Carlyle (1795–1881), Scottish author.

Personal Assessment

Before composing the final mural of your life, perhaps you should begin by sketching a light outline. Bill Bates has put together a course entitled Life Appreciation, specifically designed to teach funeral directors how to plan more personalized funerals. Clients are asked to fill out a form that includes details about their lives that are both factual and spiritual. Some of the questions include the following:

What accomplishments do you feel good about?

What are some of your fondest memories?

What people have had the greatest impact on your life?

What things would you like to do before you die?

What people would you like to say good-bye to?

If you could live your life over again,

what would you spend less time doing?

what would you spend more time doing?

What would you do if you could do anything before you die?

What are the things you always wanted to do but have not?

What behaviors and attitudes have held you back?

What behaviors and attitudes do you admire in others?

What things have given you the most pleasure in life?

What causes and beliefs are you most passionate about?

What is the most fun you have ever had?

What are you most proud of?

Thinking through the answers to these questions will give you a vivid outline from which to arrange your funeral details. Perhaps equally importantly, completing it will give you a new perspective on your life today. These and all other introspections that crop up during your funeral planning process may well help you to live more fully and realize all of your goals more completely.

The greater danger for most of us lies not in setting our aim too high and falling short, but in setting our aim too low, and achieving our mark.

—Michelangelo (1475–1564), sculptor, painter, architect, and poet.

Outline

Generally, a service has the following components:

Prelude
Introduction
Music
Life story
Music
Scripture, prayer, or readings
Words from family or friends
Music
Eulogy
Closing ceremony
Postlude

Within this general outline, you can now begin to plan your service so that it expresses your spirit. Leaving information in written form will help your loved ones to put together a beautiful service all about you.

One suggestion, based on personal experience, is not to encourage an "open mike" at your service. Although it might seem like a creative way for people to express themselves in a freeform manner, it usually does not work well. Remarks that have been thoughtfully written out and edited have a much better chance of producing an organized overall program than random remarks. At the gathering after the service, people will have an opportunity to speak and express themselves.

6. Fundamentals

Considerations

- Thoughtfully answer the suggested questions
- Review your responses as they affect your life today
- Establish a basic outline for the service

Notes

"I am as you will be"

7

Service Basics

Readings

Language exerts hidden power, like a moon on the tides.

—Rita Mae Brown (1944–), U.S. author and social activist.

Your funeral is one of the last times you will be able to communicate your personal beliefs and philosophies. The readings you choose should reflect your voice. Readings have traditionally come from the bible or other religious texts; however, anywhere you find meaningful words is fine. Poetry and verse speak volumes. Song lyrics can hold wonderful messages. There are no rules.

If you are a spiritual person, the New and Old Testaments are a treasure. The Twenty-third Psalm is seemingly always read—and perhaps with good reason. Don't throw out the baby with the bathwater.

Twenty-third Psalm

The Lord is my Shepherd: I shall not want.

He maketh me to lie down in green pastures;

He leadeth me beside the still waters, he restoreth my soul.

He leadeth me in the paths of righteousness for His name's sake,

Yea, though I walk through the valley of the shadow of death

I will fear no evil; for thou art with me;

Thy rod and Thy staff, they comfort me.

A message of support for your loved ones is a gift as well:

MISS ME, BUT LET ME GO

When I come to the end of the road
And the sun has set for me,
I want no rites in a gloom-filled room,
Why cry for a soul set free?

Miss me a little … but not too long,
And not with your head bowed low,
Remember the love that once we shared,
Miss me, but let me go.

For this is a journey that we all must take,
And each must go alone,
It's all part of the master plan,
A step on the road to home.

When you are lonely and sick of heart,
Go to the friends we know
And bury your sorrows in doing good deeds,
Miss me, but let me go.

—Anonymous

The following was printed on the Queen Mother's funeral program:

You can shed tears that she is gone
or you can smile because she has lived.

You can close your eyes and pray that she'll come back
or you can open your eyes and see all she's left.

Your heart can be empty because you can't see her
or you can be full of the love you shared.

You can turn your back on tomorrow and live yesterday
or you can be happy for tomorrow, because of yesterday.

You can remember her, and only that she's gone
or you can cherish her memory, and let it live on.

You can cry and close your mind, be empty and turn your back
or you can do what she'd want: smile, open your eyes, love and go on.

—Anonymous

Music

A song will outlive all sermons in memory.

> —Henry Giles (1814–1880), English author.

Music is the soul of language.

> —Max Heindel (1865–1919), Christian occultist and astrologer.

There is a theory that music existed even before words as a form of communication. You would be hard pressed to create as powerful an emotion with words as with music. The music you choose has the potential to dominate the entire spirit of your funeral. Music can be played before the service begins and interspersed throughout. A soloist may be asked to perform. Or you may choose to have songs sung in unison, to encourage participation. A sound system can easily accommodate any music you would like to play during the service.

There are traditional hymns that have been played for years and years at funerals, and again, with good reason. They are powerful and filled with significance. Is "Amazing Grace" overplayed? Perhaps, but it could also be argued that 1 Corinthians 13 is an overused verse at weddings. Yet these words are timeless:

Amazing grace! How sweet the sound
That saved a wretch like me!
I once was lost, but now I'm found;
Was blind, but now I see.
'Twas grace that brought me safe thus far,
And grace will lead me home.

You know what music you like and what lyrics inspire you. If the golden oldies of the fifties never quite got out of your system, then pick your favorites and play them. Remember Neil Sedaka's "Stairway to Heaven"?

> I'll build a stairway to heaven
> I'll climb to the highest star
> I'll build a stairway to heaven
> 'Cause heaven is where you are!

Broadway show tunes often have evocative words. *The Sound of Music* included "Climb Ev'ry Mountain":

> Climb ev'ry mountain,
> Ford every stream,
> Follow every rainbow
> Till you find your dream.

Does the Michigan fight song define you? Let's hear "The Victors"!

> Hail to the victors valiant, hail to the conquering heroes
> Hail! Hail! to Michigan, The champions of the west.

If country and western music flows through your veins, Joe Diffie's "Prop Me Up Beside the Jukebox" might be just the tune to make everyone remember you:

> Prop me up beside the jukebox when I die
> Lord I wanna go to heaven, but I don't wanna go tonight
> Fill my boots up with sand, put a stiff drink in my hand
> Prop me up beside the jukebox when I die.

Lee Ann Womack's "I Hope You Dance" has lyrics that leave a poignant message for people:

> I hope you still feel small when you stand beside the ocean
> Whenever one door closes I hope one more opens
> Promise me that you'll give faith a fighting chance
> And when you get the choice to sit it out or dance
> I hope you dance

Or the very simple "Rainbow Connection" might say it all for you:

Someday we'll find it, the Rainbow Connection
The lovers, the dreamers, and me.

Music is well said to be the speech of angels.
—Thomas Carlyle (1795–1881) Scottish essayist, satirist, and historian.

After silence, that which comes nearest to expressing the inexpressible is music.
—Aldous Huxley (1894–1963), British writer, Music at Night, 1931.

Funeral Procession

Even the procession to the cemetery can be memorable and resound with your spirit. One woman drove the hearse in her husband's funeral procession, because he had always insisted that she drive whenever they went out. An elderly man had walked his golden retriever, Sam, throughout his neighborhood for hours every day. Sam led his procession. There was a fellow who had driven the local ice cream truck in a small town for years. His procession was led by his ice cream truck, and free popsicles were distributed at his graveside. These departed spirits were in attendance at their respective funerals.

The service for the first man in a small New England town to lose his life in Iraq drew quite a crowd, both inside and outside the local Congregational church. After the service, his body was placed on a horse-drawn caisson. His immediate family walked directly behind the horse and was followed by hundreds of locals in a mile-long procession to the local cemetery. There were folks along the entire route waving small American flags; an enormous flag was draped over the entrance to the cemetery as well. This procession will not soon be forgotten by anyone in town.

Bob was the president of a motorcycle club. He had always instructed his friends to "make some noise" when they pulled out of his driveway. He had made arrangements for a motorcycle hearse to carry his body to the cemetery. The side-car made a detour past his house on the way to the cemetery, with twenty-five motorcycles following it. As each one passed Bob's driveway, they gunned their engines, "making some noise" as a final tribute to him.

7. Service Basics

Considerations

- Assemble favorite readings and sayings
- Formulate musical selections
- Think about your funeral procession

Notes

HERE LIES EZEKIAL AIKLE

AGE 102

THE GOOD

DIE YOUNG

Ezekial Aikle
East Dalhousie Cemetery, Nova Scotia

8

Service Enhancements

Beyond the basics of a funeral, there are a few enhancements that can greatly augment the personal touch of your service. These additions have the potential to make your thoughts and ideas stay with people long after they leave the funeral.

Life Story Line

Memory is the diary that we all carry around with us.

> —Oscar Wilde (1854–1900), Irish dramatist, novelist, and poet.

A great place to start your planning process is to put together a factual time line of your life and then fill it in with interesting pieces of information. Let's say you were born in 1935. It might be fun to include some "current events" of that particular year. Who was president? When did you get a TV? What were the lives of your parents like? Did your grandfather remember the Civil War?

Pertinent facts about your childhood and schooling are also interesting. Probably not many of the folks in attendance were with you in second grade. Did you really have to be home before the streetlights went on? You climbed *how far* up that rock? The story of how you and your husband or wife met is certainly interesting to lots of people. So many of those details from years ago shaped your life.

These memories can be woven into a meaningful piece to be read by a predetermined person at your funeral. All of these pieces of information are a part of what makes you who you are.

Personal Memories

To live in hearts we leave behind is not to die.

> —Thomas Campbell (1777–1844), Scottish poet.

Next, share some memories. Certain memories are once-in-a-lifetime events: weddings, parties, vacations, and births. But many others are those small life experiences that happened every day at some point in your life. Maybe it was a silly TV show that you watched every night with your children. Maybe it was pulling lobster traps. Maybe it was going to church on Sunday mornings. Maybe it was a pickup game of soccer on Saturday afternoons. Memories are made up of moments, not days. Recollections can be seemingly inconsequential, but on closer inspection, they are full of meaning. And all those attending your service who were a part of these memories will be remarkably touched.

The other facts that shape you are your hobbies and recreational activities. Maybe you are one of those people who can't get to the golf course fast enough whenever the occasion arises. Maybe you are on your boat in any kind of weather. Do you work on bonsai trees in your spare time or build birdhouses? Have you knitted scarves, hats, and mittens for everyone in your family? Do you make your own wine? Do you create beautiful jewelry? Do you tinker with cars? Do you play an instrument? Have you traveled to Europe, South America, and the South Pacific? Or do you just have a favorite town in northern Michigan that calls you back summer after summer? Have you always had dogs and cats? What were their names? How about that favorite sports team—do you have Chicago Cubs paraphernalia all over the house? Jot down these thoughts, to be read and to give substance to your service.

> Ann and Henry had traveled to the four corners of the Earth during their lifetimes. When Henry passed away, Ann collected a dozen matchbooks from the assortment they had collected from their travels. She placed twelve candles in the front of the church and gave matches to their twelve nieces and nephews. When she called their names, they stepped forward, read the name and location on their matchbook, and lit a candle. It was a nice way to have the family participate. Collectively, it was a wonderful tribute to their personal memories.

Humor

Comedy is simply a funny way of being serious.

—Peter Ustinov (1921–2004), English actor and author.

There are very few things in life that are not improved with a bit of humor. Your family and friends have known and loved you for a lifetime and are probably quite familiar with your brand of humor. What could be nicer than to weave a bit of this humor into your service? People want to feel your presence, and humor is so personal that you will indeed be felt.

Are you a real punster? Let people know that you were "dying" to be at this service! Always the first with a new blonde joke? Leave them with the one about the blonde who was fired from the M&M factory for throwing away all the *W*s. Laughter and tears mix well.

He deserves paradise who makes his companions laugh.

—The *Koran*, the central religious text of Islam.

Participation

The only cure for grief is action.

—George Henry Lewes (1833–1911), English society lawyer.

Participation by your family and friends is a key component to a successful funeral, and it sets the healing process in motion. Involvement gives everyone a structure to show their love. Participation also helps to define the reality of the death. Though it may seem harsh, reality turns loose the grieving and releases feelings.

People can be involved in many different ways. Ask a friend to do a eulogy. It is an honor to be asked, and it may settle much angst. You might also ask a family member or friend to read a poem or verse that you hold dear to your heart. Having been asked to read a particular piece makes a real connection. Someone might even be asked to sing or play a solo. The more personalized the service, the more it will mean and the more beneficial it will be.

At this point, it is important to note that too detailed a funeral plan can have an adverse effect. Some details should be left to the survivors, to assure their participation. Leave some wiggle room for your survivors to fine-tune your plans a bit. Thoughtful planning will allow a number of people to participate to some extent.

> When Beth's friend Karen died, she left a real void. They had walked together every day for years and had faced so many of life's ups and downs together. One of their shared joys was gardening. Each had a spectacular garden. Beth, always one to keep busy, decided to put together small bags of seeds to give everyone at the funeral service to take home and plant. Not only was it a lovely remembrance of Karen, but it served Beth well to feel that she was contributing to the service.

Do not protect yourself by a fence, but rather by your friends.

—Czech proverb

Participation by Children

When making funeral plans, it is also important to consider the children in your life, be they your grandchildren, your nieces and nephews, or your favorite little neighbor, who feeds the cat. If handled with appropriate developmental understanding, funerals experienced in childhood help children to be less afraid of death as adults.

Children should be included in a funeral service if it gives them comfort. A youngster may want to play or sing their mother's favorite song. Another may wish to recite a favorite verse. These presentations may be taped or live. It is imperative that children understand that their participation will not be judged as a measure of their love for the deceased. They need not participate in order to prove their affection. And be sure to accept a child's decision regarding participation warmly and lovingly.

Children may also help choose favorite photos for a memory board. Be aware to choose photos that portray happy times and that are ones that the child particularly likes.

Older children may wish to deliver a eulogy.

> Fran's children, Martha, Caleb, and Johnny, all spoke briefly at their father's funeral. The common message they shared was the lesson Fran had reiterated throughout his life, which was simply: "Try hard, and be nice." Although they had diverse interests and distinct personalities, all of his children described how his lesson had influenced their personal lives. Collectively, it was a brilliant tribute to Fran.

A thoughtfully planned funeral service can be a great inspiration to children. Demonstrating a life well lived is an invaluable lesson for young minds. Be aware of the young people, and include them appropriately.

Children require guidance and sympathy far more than instruction.
—Annie Sullivan (1866–1936), lifelong teacher to Helen Keller.

Ceremony

Another important component of a meaningful funeral service is ceremony. Ceremonies are powerful, and they are a wonderful way to involve people. A single candle lit by a loved one is powerful, as are numerous candles burning together to form community. Releasing butterflies or even doves has become popular, along with balloon releases. Looking up to the sky also lightens spirits.

Another idea is for someone to hand each attendee an item that holds significance for you as they arrive at your service. At some point during the service, have everyone come forward and either place this article in the casket or in a bowl or basket in the front. Collectively, these items symbolize not only you, but the connection of the community of people at your service. Ceremonies honoring a person's individuality are poignant.

> Susan was an avid gardener. She was truly at her best with dirty fingernails. Whenever she went anywhere, she inevitably had a beautiful bunch of flowers to give away. As people entered into Susan's service, each was handed a beautiful flower. At the close of the ceremony people were asked to place their flowers on Susan's coffin to form a final, beautiful bouquet.

Traditions

If you have certain traditions that are distinctly yours, incorporate them into your service. Sharing these rituals can be incredibly evocative. Consider carefully what would best convey your spirit to your family and friends.

> Marilyn was widowed after sixty years of marriage. She confided to her minister that she and her husband had always held hands and said the *Lord's Prayer* together at the end of each day. At the conclusion of the service, Marilyn was escorted to the casket, where she placed her hand over her husband's, and the entire congregation stood and recited the *Lord's Prayer* with her.

8. Service Enhancements

Considerations

- Weave a life story line
- Describe personal memories
- Incorporate some humor
- Include participation of loved ones
- Create some sort of ceremony
- Focus on traditions

Notes

Henry David Thoreau
Concord, Massachusetts 1862

9

Service Accessories

The "coup de grâce" for your funeral is to put your personal stamp on all of the visuals. Perhaps you haunted a local coffee shop every morning. By setting out a copy of "your" daily newspaper, along with "your" coffee mug, with a photo that was taken one morning with you and all your morning friends, people will almost see you, as they listen to your last thoughts.

Location, Location, Location

So, if you are not required to have your funeral in an unfamiliar, cavernous church or a dingy parlor with brocade chairs in a dark funeral home, the choices already seem better, don't they? Since your funeral is your own personal event, its location takes on a whole new meaning. If you are a hiker who loves the outdoors, maybe there is a spot along the Appalachian Trail that would be a lovely place for your family and friends to gather. Or perhaps your home is your castle, and you have worked and reworked every square inch of it. Wouldn't it be lovely to have everyone gathered right there? An avid gardener might be best felt in the midst of flowering grounds. And if you will be most vividly felt in your lifelong church, most assuredly hold it there. Gather your friends and family where you belong.

Brian had been a zookeeper for his entire life. His real passion in life had been working with the animals. When Brian passed away, friends and family were invited to gather in a tent outside the zoo gates for a cocktail reception. They then boarded a waiting train and began a slow ride around the zoo, stopping at the bear pavilion, the lion pavilion, and finally at the arboretum. At each stop, photographs that Brian had taken of the various animals were on display, and his wife and best friends gave meditations about Brian and his life. Nowhere was Brian's presence felt more than at his zoo.

Flowers

Earth laughs in flowers.

> —Ralph Waldo Emerson (1803–1882), U.S. essayist and poet.

Flowers are another very personal choice. If your friends walk in and see the tricolor carnations you always found abhorrent, they will not only think you are not there, they will hope you are not there. Don't let it happen. If you want irises, sunflowers, roses, or daisies, include that preference in your preparations, and your wishes will be fulfilled. Planning a tropical theme? Include a palm tree.

Etiquette pages now have questions such as, "Is it proper to have a color theme for a funeral?" It is your funeral. If you want to have a gentle white surrounding everyone, all-white flowers will set the tone. If you are more of a purple person, specify just exactly how many irises you want. Flowers define so much.

Bread feeds the body, indeed, but flowers feed also the soul.

> —Mohammad (c. 571–652), prophet of Islam.

Props

The charm of fishing is that it is the pursuit of what is elusive but attainable, a perpetual series of occasions for hope.

> —John Buchan (1875–1940), Scottish author and politician.

What do your fly-fishing rod and hand-tied flies express about you? Props are becoming more and more popular at funeral services. A single item can say a great deal about you. You are "there" when people see a beautiful quilt you made, your toy poodle in the front row, your favorite hat, a shirt with your favorite team's logo, or a basket of flowers from your garden. Those who knew you will see these items and feel you as well. They are powerful tools and can be used extremely well.

Photos: Worth a Thousand Words

Photography does not create eternity, as art does; it embalms time.

> —Andre Bazin (1918–1958), French film critic.

Pictures are a wonderful tool for reminiscing. They are a glimpse of who you were, where you were, and with whom you spent your time. Good photos capture your very essence.

You may take the time now to select favorite photos of yourself to be used on a picture board. One consideration, however, is that collecting these photos can actually be very therapeutic for your family and friends when you are gone. These people need to participate in some aspects of your funeral plan. Perhaps consolidating old photos would be a cathartic exercise for them at this time. And even if you do hand-pick all of your favorite photos, there is no guarantee that they will not include the one of you sopping wet, pulling yourself back into the boat.

A collection of photos can also be made into a video. There are businesses that specialize in putting together video portraits, as they have come to be known. These folks will assemble your selected photos in any sequence you desire, and then put them to music. And, of course, you can choose the music as well. Another, more costly alternative is to make a video starring you … as you. You can put together a staff to do a video of yourself, including an original script, professional actors, and animation, for a mere $75,000. If this is your style, go for it.

> *A photograph is a most important document, and there is nothing more damning to go down to posterity than a silly, foolish smile caught and fixed forever.*
>
> —Mark Twain (1835–1910), American humorist.

Program

Whether you are in a church, on a mountainside, or gathered in a garden, a printed program makes people more comfortable. This agenda helps those present at the service to be more at ease, knowing the order of what is to come. At this point, you will have made many personal decisions about elements of the service, and this compilation makes your wishes quite clear. The program may need to be tweaked somewhat, depending on circumstances, but you can certainly create the bulk of it.

The program gives you another opportunity to include any thoughts you might want to share. These may be personal thoughts or quotations you have found meaningful. A short quotation says so much. What fun, to be on the lookout for meaningful phrases to be left on a program encompassing your life!

You may choose your favorite photos for the front and back of the program. Selecting these all-important photos is another moment that can quickly put your life into perspective. Which photos are most important? Why are they important, and what can be done to recreate more of these moments? Start taking more of those photos now.

In Lieu of …

To give away money is an easy matter and any man's power. But to decide to whom to give it and how much and when, for what purpose and how, is neither in every man's power, nor an easy matter.

—Aristotle (384 B.C.–322 B.C.), Greek philosopher.

Another consideration is whether you want people to send flowers as a memorial to you, or to have the money directed elsewhere. Donations can be made to various medical organizations, a hospice, or a scholarship fund. Money may be directed toward a school, a library, or any worthwhile civic organization. Or if you want your loved ones to be surrounded by beautiful flowers, that's your choice.

Invitations

If you are planning to have a memorial service, and if time permits, you may wish to see to one last detail. Perhaps you have always prided yourself on your unique invitations. Your funeral could be a meaningful opportunity to create a final summons. Try to project yourself to that time when your friends and family will be gathering to celebrate your life. A spirited or thought-provoking quotation certainly could serve as an introduction. The time and place may be left blank, and you can leave a "guest list" for mailing. It also serves as an opportunity to acknowledge and thank all those who attend. The invitation can be very compelling.

A THANK YOU INVITATION

The question is not whether we will die, but how we will live.

—Joan Borysenko

A Final Life Celebration

Time:
Place:

Please know that I have loved my life.
And what is to love in life but family and friends?
Therefore, I thank you from the bottom of my heart.

JOIN ME FOR MY FINAL PARTY

It's not that I'm afraid to die, I just don't want to be there when it happens.

—Woody Allen

I Was Dying to Be Here, but ...

Time:
Place:

That is the best—to laugh with someone because you think the same things are funny.

—Gloria Vanderbilt

Thanks, everyone! I'll miss you.

9. Service Accessories

Considerations

- Choose a location for your service
- Assemble your favorite flowers
- Select personal props as reminders
- Put together a nice assortment of photographs
- Create a program
- Define your donation choice
- Think about writing an invitation

Notes

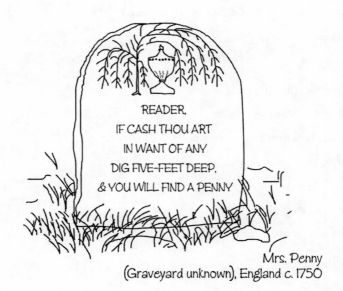

READER,
IF CASH THOU ART
IN WANT OF ANY
DIG FIVE-FEET DEEP,
& YOU WILL FIND A PENNY

Mrs. Penny
(Graveyard unknown), England c. 1750

10

Afterparty

The informal gathering after the service is where the most healing takes place. People are one-on-one, sharing their stories and memories. Here is where tears and laughter are intermixed. So it is important that your presence be felt, for it will bring comfort as people share their feelings.

Many of the components previously suggested for your funeral service can be incorporated at this gathering. The formal service may be at a church, and the reception may be in a meadow. Having two segments allows you to express yourself in multiple ways.

Your Favorite Fare

A passage from *Being Dead Is No Excuse,* a novel about funerals in the Mississippi Delta, describes traditional reception menus in that area:

> You can't bury a self-respecting Deltan without certain foods. Chief among these is tomato aspic with homemade mayonnaise—without which you practically can't get a death certificate—closely followed by Aunt Hebe's Coconut Cake, and Virginia's Butterbeans. "You get the best food at funerals," we always say, and it's true. Funeral procedure is something that we all just know. A legion of friends working behind the scenes, coordinating the food, makes sure the essential Delta death foods are represented in sufficient quantities.

Lacking these ironclad traditions, you should plan and create your own personal menu. Pull out all the stops. Serve your favorite foods. Do you have favorite recipes? Ask someone to prepare and dish them up. Do you make your own beer? Lay in a supply, and have it served. Is the mushroom and pepperoni pizza from your local House of Pizza your favorite meal every Friday night? Order takeout. If you enjoy entertaining formally, arrange to have an event with white linens, silver, candles, your preferred delicacies, and a lovely wine. Your friends and family will most assuredly feel you there. People are identified with their culinary choices.

Bud loved to barbeque. He had a few favorite recipes that were all his own. Even his sauce had its own distinct smell. After Bud's service, everyone gathered in his backyard, cranked up the grill, and cooked up all his favorite dishes, even using the recipe for his own personal sauce. Bud was missed, but Bud was felt.

Setting

Hold this event where people can sense your presence. Is there a particular beach or hiking trail that you especially love? Meet there, and have a picnic. Were you the harbormaster for years and years? Gather on the dock, around the boat. Perhaps you could arrange for an assembly at the bird sanctuary that you helped to preserve. If your real joy was spending time with your friends at a local pub, by all means, have folks gather there and feel your spirit. If you love to tinker and the garage is your second home, you might want to convene in the driveway. Just make it yours.

When Tammy's grandmother died, the fitting memorial for her was clear. For years, each Sunday, she had made her family one of her delicious Sunday dinners. At one o'clock the next Sunday afternoon, her family gathered at her home and ate Sunday dinner together. Each family made one of her celebrated dishes. The combined aromas captured her spirit as perhaps nothing else could. Even her silverware and dishes were reminiscent of her. Her home, her dishes, her food … she was there.

Music

Play your favorite music. Particularly if you held back and used more traditional music at your service, this is your opportunity to really do it! Ask that a jazz group play at this event. Or perhaps a great fiddler could infuse your spirit into the reception. Play chamber music. Put together a CD with your favorite tunes now. You can enjoy it and update it as time progresses, and it will be ready for your celebration.

Katie was a country music buff. If it twanged and rocked, she loved it! She was constantly putting together mixes of her current favorites. When folks gathered after her service, those collections were played. The sweet country tunes added a personal note for everyone.

Keepsakes

Perhaps akin to a "goodie bag," a small and meaningful keepsake can be a wonderful addition to this gathering. It is probably best kept to a very simple memento, but clearly, it should be one with meaning.

Dave was an avid golfer. His wife, MaryAnn, gave each person at his service a gleaming new golf ball. She asked that each of them take the ball out on a beautiful sunny day, tee it up, and smack it off, in memory of Dave.

Lenore loved beautiful shells and combed the beach throughout her entire lifetime, collecting unique conches, sand dollars, and periwinkles. She left a basket filled with her favorites and requested that each guest at her service take one as a remembrance.

The gathering after your service is really very important. Make yourself felt.

10. Afterparty

Considerations

- Choose the menu
- Select an appropriate setting
- Decide what music to use
- Put together small keepsakes

Notes

11

Obituaries

I wake up every morning at nine and grab for the morning paper. Then I look at the obituary page. If my name is not on it, I get up.

—Benjamin Franklin (1706–1790), American statesman.

You probably thought that the essay you wrote for your college application was the most important one you would ever write. That was a bit premature. The big one comes at the end—your obituary.

Obituaries come in many sizes and styles. One may be the simple facts delineating your life events. Another might be a bit more personal and include lists of relatives. Some are witty. Most importantly, however, an obituary should cover the aspects of your life that matter most to you. Perhaps you were an All-Star football player. While that is a major accomplishment, perhaps the fact that you volunteered at a local summer camp, coaching children's football teams, is what you truly wish to be remembered for. And although you might have headed a prestigious law firm that guided some of the most esteemed financial institutions through convoluted negotiations, your hand-tied flies could be what you deem to be your greatest accomplishment. Your loved ones will never know if you don't tell them.

Obituaries have become the focus of a new cult, as witnessed by the formation of the Great Obituary Writers' Conference. These annual conferences attract the authors of these final tributes, as well as obituary junkies, who are obsessed with reading them each day. Obituaries have become a literary art form.

Your obituary, however, will hopefully have more substance than mere fodder for intellectual wit. A first-rate obituary will, in a few words, capture the spirit of your whole life. The likelihood of a random reporter, regardless of his abilities, divining your soul in a short article seems fairly remote. Time to put pen to paper, or fingers to keyboard, and compose your own obituary.

Obituary Realities

Obituaries appear routinely in large, prominent newspapers, in local daily newspapers, and in community weekly papers. The obituaries of a select few appear in metropolitan newspapers, and they are most often included due to the prestige of the deceased, a quirk in the life of the deceased, or just plain old good timing. If you were a state senator, the last widow of a soldier from the Civil War, or gobbled up by a vagrant shark on a New Jersey beach, you are almost guaranteed a prominent obituary. Your chances are also improved if it is a slow news day without too many celebrities sharing the limelight. Lacking these criteria, however, you probably will not have a full-blown obituary in a major newspaper, but you are assured of being included in your smaller regional paper.

Death notices are featured regularly in larger newspapers. These pieces are usually concise and, as a rule, merely factual, since they are rather expensive. An average abbreviated death notice in a metropolitan newspaper runs about $200 per day—not an occasion for verbose prose. Investigate your local papers, and settle on a budget and content for your death notice and for your local obituary. It will not only be about you, but by you.

Content

The brass tacks of obituaries are pretty consistent. A quick perusal of obituaries in a reputable newspaper will give you those details. The essential facts concerning your relatives, educational accomplishments, occupational history, and special recommendations are customary. The date and cause of death will probably have to be completed by others.

The real heart of your obituary is yours to create. A good obituary will speak to each and every one of your accomplishments. A great obituary will reveal a small detail or vignette that captures your real inner self. Perhaps you have been married to the same woman for over fifty-two years. If you go on to say that you brought her a cup of tea in bed every morning, that reveals so much more. These are the facts that capture your essence.

The "Portraits of Grief" that were published by the *New York Times* after 9/11 are an excellent example of characterizing a personality in a few short words. A new form of obituary was a necessity after this terrible tragedy, as it seemed impossible to write traditional obituaries for the numerous victims. In his biographical mini-profiles, Jon Landman captured the personalities of almost 1,600 individual people using emblematic, usually endearing anecdotes. Reading these abbreviated yet inspiring obituaries might spark your imagination and lead you to redefine your most important moments. Here is one example:

March 9, 2003
Mario Santoro: Good Food, Good Company

Yes, Mario Santoro was a dedicated emergency medical technician who loved his job. Yes, he doted on his daughter, Sofia, who is now 3. And yes, he was a passionate volunteer basketball coach at his local church who sometimes showed up to practice after catching only an hour or two of sleep, after a late shift on the job.

But those who knew him best also realized that Mr. Santoro, 28, loved, more than almost anything else, to have a great meal with close friends and family.

Steak. Seafood. Appetizers. Good wine, good beer. It almost didn't matter what was on the table, as long as the food was good and the company divine, said his widow, Léonor Ramos-Santoro.

"It was kind of like breathing for him; it was almost religious for him, like taking care of your soul," she said about her husband, who immigrated from Argentina as a young boy. "Meals were sacred. You sit down and you enjoy. You're not caught up in what's going on outside."

Sometimes the Santoros made their way to the Bridge Cafe, a restaurant not far from their apartment in Lower Manhattan. At home, Mr. Santoro relished his wife's arroz con gandules, or rice with pigeon peas, with an extra zing of garlic.

"For the rest of my life, I will want Mario to come home for a meal," she said. "If he has to go back, then fine, go back. But just one more meal, that's all."

Benefits

If you sit down and begin writing your own obituary, it is almost guaranteed that you will gain an immeasurable perspective on your life. The composing, in itself, is cathartic. If you want an interesting and meaningful obituary, you will have to employ some form of fiction or live an interesting and meaningful life. Bingo.

Imagine what it would be like to see your own obituary.

In 1888 a French newspaper wrote an obituary with the headline "The Merchant of Death has Died." A fellow named Alfred was reading this article, which went on to describe how the deceased had invented dynamite, one of the world's most destructive forces. As it turned out, the obituary had been written about the wrong man. The obituary was meant to be for Ludvig, Alfred's brother. Alfred himself was the man who had invented dynamite, and he was most distressed to see his life capsulated in this fashion. Alfred was an accomplished scientist with more than 350 other patents; he also wrote poetry and drama. As a pacifist, efforts to promote peace were of paramount importance to him. Alfred's surname was Nobel.

He went on to establish and fund the Nobel Peace Prize. It has been suggested that reading this mistaken obituary was the impetus for his establishing this award.

Writing and previewing your own obituary can shed an interesting light on your life.

11. Obituaries

Considerations

- Read and become familiar with obituaries
- Investigate likely sources to publish your obituary
- Write a concise death notice, leaving appropriate details blank
- Consider which of your life accomplishments you want to emphasize
- Choose a vignette from your life that captures your spirit
- Write your obituary

Notes

SHE ALWAYS SAID
HER FEET WERE KILLING HER
BUT NOBODY BELIEVED HER

Hollywood Cemetery, Richmond, Virginia

12

Ethical Wills

What you have learned is as valuable as what you have earned.

—Susan B. Trumbull, founder of Personal Legacy Advisors.

A legal will is to your ethical will as a photo is to a painting. The photo depicts a scene in precise, accurate detail. A painting, however, is a more subjective and intuitive representation of the same scene. An ethical will bequeaths values rather than valuables. Rather than telling your loved ones what you are leaving them, it tells them what you want them to know.

Legal Wills vs. Ethical Wills

Clearly, a legal will is a necessity. Increasingly, however, ethical wills are being recognized as equally valuable. This document imparts moral and religious values, lessons learned in life, and hopes and wishes for loved ones. An ethical will rises to a transcendent state.

Written ethical wills were in existence in medieval times, and they survive today with the same basic goal of passing on knowledge to future generations. They leave, in written form, those ideas and values to which you most closely ascribe. The goal is for you to leave a spiritual legacy to those left behind. Ideally, the ethical will serves as a window into your soul.

An ethical will works well in conjunction with your legal will, as it can both clarify and justify the logic behind decisions in the legal document. This document can also alleviate any confusion or misunderstandings, by giving an explanation of potentially controversial components of your legal will. If money is being left to an organization or charity, it is valuable for the heirs to understand the motives behind this donation. Again, your values are the focus of these explanations.

Unsolicited Advice

If you have given sums of money to your heirs in your legal will, you might make use of your ethical will to dispense advice concerning its use. There are two fields of thought on including counsel. One assumes that the money is a gift and therefore may be used as the recipient sees fit. The other believes that donors are entitled to clarify their wishes or hopes for the funds. Weigh your decisions carefully.

One must know not just how to accept a gift, but with what grace to share it.

—Maya Angelou (1928–), American poet.

Family History

An ethical will can also describe your family's history. As people become increasingly mobile, the old family stories are being lost in verbal form. The stories and personal events of your life—your accomplishments and disappointments—can be quite helpful to future generations. The sooner these stories are recorded permanently, the greater their chance of survival far into the future.

Writing Your Ethical Will

The length of your ethical will is your personal choice. The content may vary from 250 pages to two and a half paragraphs. Try not to let too many words dilute your content.

Some people have a difficult time getting started and find it easier to record their ethical will in video form. At some point, you should transcribe the content to written form, as there is no guarantee that the future will include equipment for playing a particular recording format.

A mini-industry has sprung up to assist people in putting together their ethical wills. These companies will interview you and put together a great variety of finished products. There are also excellent books to help guide you through this exercise on your own. Try to write on acid-free or archival paper—ideally, this legacy will last for years to come.

Periodically update your ethical will as additional insights occur to you. You must also decide when to share this document with your loved ones. Often it is beneficial to present it to them before you die, as it is almost certain to evoke some meaningful discussions. Or it may be kept in a safe spot, with other legal documents.

Potential Damage

Another important aspect of an ethical will is to be aware of the damage any negative comments may have on survivors. Once you are dead, you cannot retract anything you say. Choose your words carefully and thoughtfully.

Benefits

Both legal wills and ethical wills impart a sense of control. Knowing that your affairs, both financial and spiritual, are in order gives a sense of peace and a feeling of closure. One type of will assures that your worldly goods will be in the proper hands, and the other allows you to live on in the hearts and minds of your loved ones. Research has even shown that writing about emotionally significant and meaningful topics can be beneficial to your health.

Another positive effect of writing an ethical will is that you will gain perspective on your present life and values. This reexamination of what you have learned in your lifetime, and the importance of certain values, forces you to confront yourself. If shared with others, it also compels you to "walk the talk" and potentially live a better life.

Dear Ben and Charlie,

Although I am in great shape, with no more adverse medical conditions than an occasional wounded knee when playing soccer, it occurs to me that time is passing, and there are a few important issues I want to make clear. In a few years, I will be retiring from commercial lobstering. I know that both of you have other plans for your future and will not be pulling lobster traps from the sea. You have both made me proud in so many ways. I respect and admire all your choices.

As you know, my grandfather and father were both lobstermen and lived in our little house on the harbor. Although it appears that you will both be in the city, pursuing your artistic and business endeavors, I hope that you will hold onto the house and use it in the summer as a family vacation house. Bring your children to swim, sail, and smell the fresh salt air. It pleases me to think of the house still being enjoyed by our family.

Love, Dad

If they're willing to take my property, they should at least be willing to consider my values.

—Rabbi Jack Rieme, writer and editor.

12. Ethical Wills

Considerations

- Consider what moral values you wish to leave behind as a legacy
- Clarify your legal will with your ethical will
- Evaluate what is reasonable advice to include in your ethical will
- Put together a family history
- Choose a vehicle to record your ethical will
- Reexamine any negative thoughts
- Decide when to share your ethical will with others

Notes

HERE RESTS IN
HONORED GLORY
AN AMERICAN
SOLDIER

UNKNOWN BUT TO GOD

LEST WE FORGET

Tomb of the Unknown Soldier

Conclusion

It is a sad weakness, after all, that the thought of a man's death hallows him anew to us; as if life were not sacred, too.

—George Eliot (1819–1880), English novelist.

You have made choices throughout your entire lifetime that have defined your being, and your end is certainly no time to leave things to chance. Your last chapter on Earth should reflect your personal dignity. At the final celebration of your life, your very presence should saturate the room. Ideally, those attending will depart having learned something about living a fuller and more meaningful life, through your recollections and life choices. This event should be life-affirming for all your loved ones.

Hopefully, planning your final life celebration will lead you on a serendipitous journey that will give you a fresh perspective on your life thus far. Is skiing down a mountaintop covered in soft, white powder your utopia? Or would you prefer to be inert on a lounge chair sunken in white sands, sipping something cool? Perhaps discovering a new species of birds in a remote section of South Africa is your ideal. Have at it! Go skiing, flop onto a beach chair, or make a reservation on South African Airlines. Be uncommonly diligent in embracing those you love and having fun with them. It is imperative to commemorate as many of life's events as possible. Be it a birthday, an anniversary, a graduation, or a full moon, gather those you love, and celebrate with them.

Again, remember that your funeral is *about* you, but *for* the living. If you have written your preferences for every little detail of your funeral, that's great. However, you should make it clear that it is acceptable to you if there are a few things the folks left behind want to tweak to make them more comfortable. It will probably affect them more than you.

I am a big believer in planning my own birthday parties. I don't like to leave those details to others. I know what I want, and I like to have it done just the way I want. Consider, for instance, the man who carefully planned his wife's fiftieth birthday party. He called all her friends, made arrangements for a beautiful hall, ordered all the right food, and even arranged for a live band. At the last minute, he called his wife's mother, who lived out of town. She was not well, but he decided to see if there was some way she might be able to attend the event. She regretted that she had to decline, but she observed that it certainly was going to be a surprise for her daughter, because it was actually her forty-ninth birthday! Don't leave a once-in-a-lifetime event to chance. Plan.

Each life ends with some sort of punctuation. Not terribly noteworthy is the common period. Been there, done it, the end. A question mark seems unfulfilling and perhaps a bit disappointing. Just what *have* I been doing all these years? The feelings surrounding an exclamation point seem like the winner to me. Yes! Fabulous! You go, girl/boy! Very, very nice! Although maybe Gracie Allen had it right when she told George Burns that her life was going to end with a comma.

Do not fear death so much, but rather the inadequate life.

—Bertolt Brecht (1898–1956), German playwright and poet.

Parable of the Twins

Once upon a time, twin boys were conceived in the same womb. Weeks passed, and the twins developed. As their awareness grew, they laughed for joy: "Isn't it great that we were conceived? Isn't it great to be alive?"

Together the twins explored their world. When they found their mother's cord that gave them life, they sang for joy: "How great is our mother's cord that she shares her own life with us?"

As weeks stretched into months, the twins noticed how much each was changing. "What does it mean?" asked the one.

"It means that our stay in this world is drawing to an end," said the other one.

"But I don't want to go," said the other one. "I want to stay here always."

"We have no choice," said the other one. "But maybe there is life after birth!"

"But how can there be?" responded the one. "We will shed our life cord, and how is life possible without it? Besides, we have seen evidence that others were here before us, and none of them have returned to tell us that there is life after birth. No, this is the end."

And so the one fell into deep despair, saying, "If conception ends in birth, what is the purpose of life in the womb? It's meaningless! Maybe there is no mother after all."

"But there has to be," protested the other. "How else did we get here? How do we remain alive?"

"Have you ever seen our mother?" said the one. "Maybe she lives only in our minds. Maybe we made her up because the idea made us feel good."

And so the last days in the womb were filled with deep questioning and fear. Finally, the moment of birth arrived.

When the twins had passed from their world, they opened their eyes and they cried. For what they saw exceeded their fondest dreams.

References

Baines, Barry K. *Ethical Wills.* (http://www.ethicalwill.com)

Bates, Bill. *Life Appreciation Training.* (http://www.lifeappreciation.com)

Baum, Rachel R., ed. *Funeral and Memorial Service Readings, Poems and Tributes.* Jefferson, North Carolina: McFarland and Company, Inc., 1999.

Baxter, Denise. *The Blue Light Coffin Co.* (http://www.bluelightcoffins.com)

Carlson, Lisa. *Caring for Your Own Dead: Your Final Act of Love.* Hinesburg, Vermont: Upper Access Books, 1998.

Cochrane, Don S. *Simply Essential Funeral Planning Kit.* Bellingham, Washington: Self-Counsel Press, 2002.

Copeland, Cyrus M., ed. *Farewell, Godspeed.* New York: Harmony Books, 2003.

Grollman, Earl A. *Living When a Loved One Has Died.* Boston: Beacon Press, 1977.

Hogan, Pat. *Alison's Gift.* Silver Spring, Maryland: Nosila Publishing, 1999.

James, Malcolm and Victoria Lynn. *Last Wishes.* Valley Forge, Pennsylvania: Mavami, Inc., 2000.

Kubler-Ross, Elisabeth. *On Death and Dying.* New York: Scribner, 1969.

Lamont, Corliss. *A Humanist Funeral Service.* Amherst, New York: Prometheus Books, 1977.

Llewellyn, John F. *Saying Goodbye Your Way.* Glendale, California: Tropico Press, 2004.

Manning, Doug. *The Funeral.* Oklahoma City, Oklahoma: In-Sight Books, 2001.

Metcalfe, Gayden and Charlotte Hays. *Being Dead Is No Excuse.* New York: Miramax Books, 2005.

Moderow, Karen. *The Parting.* Alpharetta, Georgia: Jordan West Publications, 1996.

Power, Dale L. and Jeffrey B. Snyder. *Do-It-Yourself Tombstones & Other Markers.* Atglen, Pennsylvania: Schiffer Publishing Company, 1999.

Power, Dale L. *Fancy Coffins to Make Yourself.* Atglen, Pennsylvania: Schiffer Publishing Company, 2001.

Ramp, Stefanie. "A Green Way of Dying," *Advocate Weekly Newspapers*, 1999. (http://www.newmassmedia.com/spring99/dying.html)

Schaeffer, Garry. *A Labor of Love.* San Diego, California: GMS Publishing, 1998.

Seaburg, Carl, ed. *Great Occasions.* Boston: Skinner House Books, 1998.

Shushan, E. R. *Grave Matters.* New York: Ballantine Books, 1990.

Siegel, Marvin, ed. *The Last Word.* New York: William Morrow and Company, 1997.

Sublette, Kathleen and Martin Flagg. *Final Celebrations.* Ventura, California: Pathfinder Publisher of California, 1992.

Turnbull, Susan B. *The Wealth of Your Life.* Wenham, Massachusetts: Benedict Press, 2005. (http://www.yourethicalwill.com)

Willson, Jane Wynne. *Funerals Without God.* Amherst, New York: Prometheus Books, 1990.

York, Sarah. *Remembering Well.* San Francisco: Jossey-Bass, 2000.

Videos

A Cemetery Special. Pittsburgh: WQED Multimedia, 2005.

A Family Undertaking. Boston: Fanlight Productions, 2004. (http://www.pbs.org/pov/pofv2004/afamilyundertaking)

Online References

Casket Furniture (http://www.casketfurniture.com)

Casket Xpress (http://www.casketxpress.com)

Costco Caskets (http://www.costco.com)

Cremation Association of North America (http://www.cremationassociation.org)

Crossings (http://www.crossings.org)

Dictionary of Quotations (http://www.quotationsreference.com)

Everlasting Memories, Inc. (http://www.evrmemories.com)

Final Passages (http://www.finalpassages.org)

Funeral Planning (http://www.funeralplan.com)

Funerals: A Consumer Guide (http://www.ftc.gov/bcp/conline/pubs/services/funeral.htm)

Glendale Memorial Nature Preserve (http://www.glendalenaturepreserve.org)

Heaven on Earth (http://www.freespace.virgin.net/heaven.earth)

Hollywood Forever Cemetery (http://www.hollywoodforevercemetery.com)

In-Sight Books: Celebrants (http://www.insightbooks.com/celebrants.aspx)

International Order of the Golden Rule (http://www.ogr.org)

Internet Cremation Society (http://www.cremation.org)

Life Legacy Foundation (http://www.lifelegacy.org)

Military Funeral Honors (http://www.militaryfuneralhonors.osd.mil/)

National Funeral Directors Association (http://www.nfda.org)

North House Folk School (http://www.northhouse.org)

Quotations Page (http://www.quotationspage.com)

Quote Land (http://www.quoteland.com)

Selected Independent Funeral Homes (http://www.selectedfuneralhomes.org)

Space Services, Incorporated (http://www.spaceservicesinc.com)

Trappist Caskets (http://www.trappistcaskets.com)

Guide for Book Club Discussions

Here are some suggested topics to spark conversations among book groups. These suggestions vary to accommodate groups that employ a strict literary analysis as well as those who discuss more personal responses. Enjoy, and rest assured: everyone has opinions on these topics.

1. Why do you think it is so difficult for people in our society to discuss death and funerals?

2. Consider both good and not-so-good funerals that you have attended. Discuss the differences.

3. How has this book changed your perspective on funerals?

4. Have you ever had to organize a funeral "cold turkey" for a loved one? Was it difficult, and why?

5. How would you anticipate using this book? Is there one aspect that you would act upon sooner, rather than later?

6. Discuss the pros and cons of sharing an ethical will with loved ones while you are still with them.

7. What particular vignette would you like someone to tell at your funeral? How does it define your spirit?

8. Discuss your obituary, and describe what important details you would like included.

9. List your three most important successes, and describe how you would creatively incorporate them into your funeral.

10. What aspect of your funeral do you think would be the most personal?

11. What are the most compelling reasons for planning your funeral?

12. When considering your personal regrets, do you feel it might be possible to rectify any situations now?

About the Author

Betty Breuhaus loves a good party—a celebration of any event, be it a birthday, a graduation, or a full moon. So what might appear as a preoccupation with death actually stems from her love of celebrations.

Recognizing that a funeral is indeed the final celebration of a life, she began a fascinating journey, exploring styles, traditions, and options for funeral services. She began with innumerable hits on Amazon.com, hours of Googling, and extensive research in the library at Mt. Ida College, New England's foremost institution for funeral service education. Numerous interviews with funeral directors, ministers, and certified celebrants followed. She also attended a Life Appreciation course for funeral directors led by Bill Bates, and she earned a celebrant certificate from a training led by Doug Manning of In-Sight Institute. Just sharing stories with family and friends turned out to be both heartening and inspirational. The path had an interesting tangent when she found that the planning process itself garnered great insights and fresh perspectives on life's great joys.

Betty Breuhaus lives with her family and dogs in Marblehead, Massachusetts.

978-0-595-43030-7
0-595-43030-9